Piano

DEVIL'S DANCE

From THE WITCHES OF EASTWICK

For Solo Violin and Piano

JOHN WILLIAMS

ISBN 978-0-634-01455-0

Visit Hal Leonard Online at
www.halleonard.com

HAL•LEONARD®
CORPORATION
7777 W. BLUEMOUND RD. P.O. BOX 13819 MILWAUKEE, WI 53213

for Gil Shaham

DEVIL'S DANCE

From THE WITCHES OF EASTWICK

JOHN WILLIAMS

Dance Diabolique (♩. = 124–128)

8vb‑ ‑ ‑ ‑ ‑ ‑ ‑ ‑

8

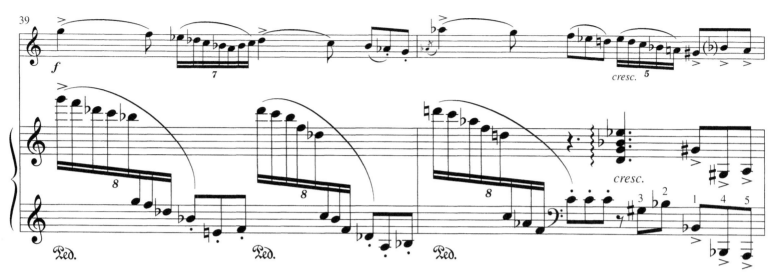

DEVIL'S DANCE

From THE WITCHES OF EASTWICK

For Solo Violin and Piano

JOHN WILLIAMS

ISBN 978-0-634-01455-0

Visit Hal Leonard Online at
www.halleonard.com

7777 W. BLUEMOUND RD. P.O. BOX 13819 MILWAUKEE, WI 53213

2

for Gil Shaham

DEVIL'S DANCE
From THE WITCHES OF EASTWICK

VIOLIN

JOHN WILLIAMS

Violin

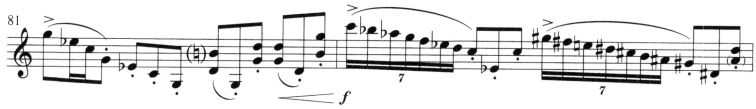

Violin

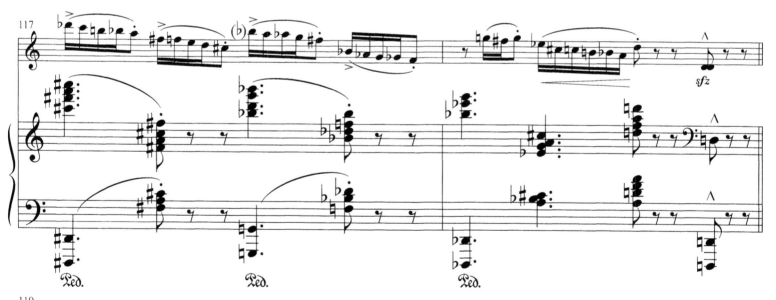